GW01606099

PINS
KNITTING PATTERNS
VILLANDOOL
WOOL

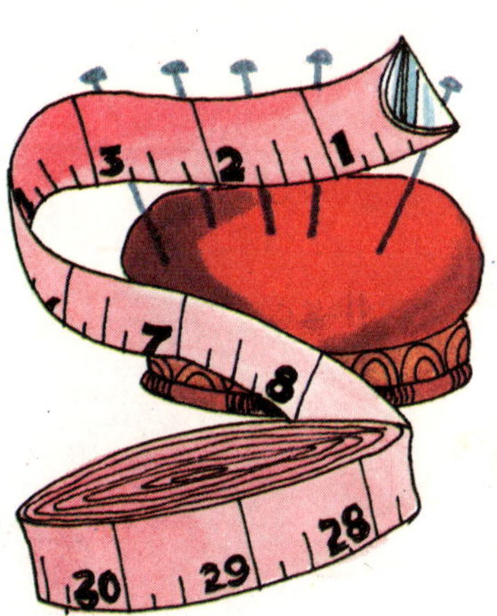

My First 'Show Me How' KNITTING BOOK

Written by Judith Dine
Illustrated by Jan Howarth
Photographs by Reg Morrison

For June

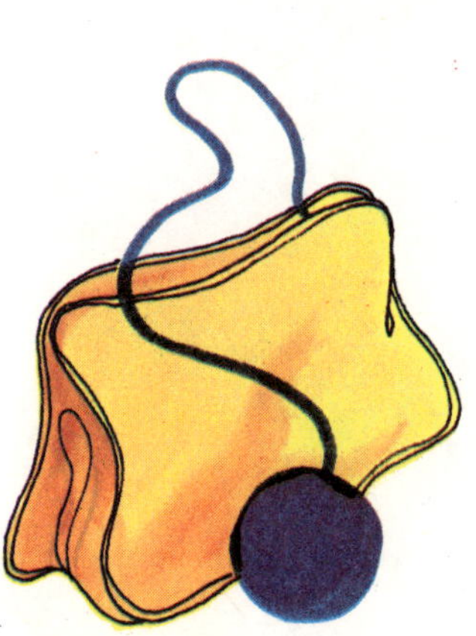

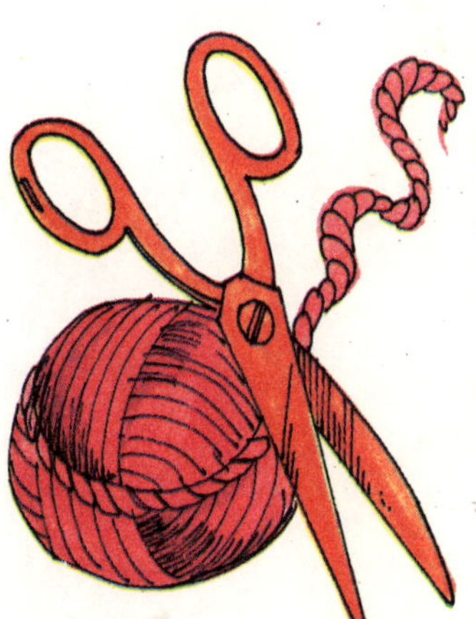

Contents

This edition published by Dean & Son Ltd., 1981
ISBN 0-603-00259-5

Text and illustrations previously published in *My First Knitting Book* and *Cooking, Knitting, Sewing for Girls*

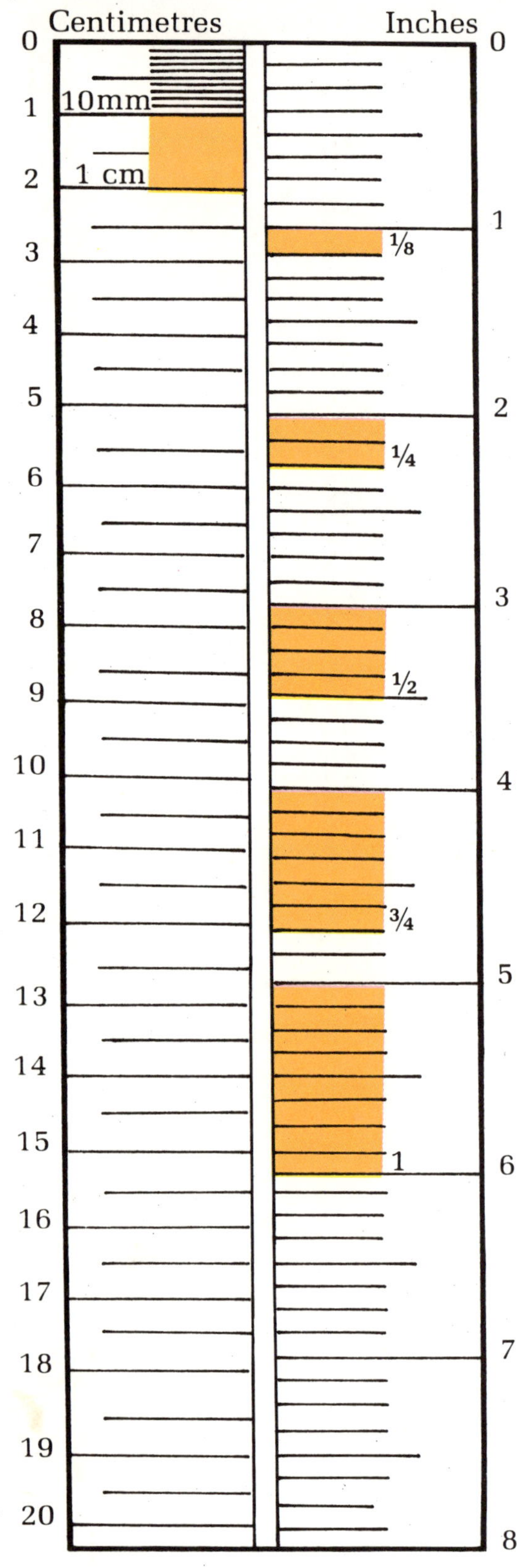

Introduction

Knitting is a very old craft that began 1,500 years ago, and since then millions of girls all over the world have spent many happy hours knitting various items.

There are many interesting designs in this book including dolls' clothes, toys, shoulder bag, scarf hat and many other items for you to knit for yourself or as a gift for a friend.

You must, however, start at the beginning and follow the simple word and picture instructions before you try to read any of the patterns.

Use up any scraps of yarn you have and practise the basic knitting stitches until you are ready to buy the Marriner yarn necessary to make the item you have chosen.

All our knitting pattern measurements are given in metric and imperial measures. We have included an exact drawing of a special ruler showing centimetres and millimetres on one side and inches on the other. If your ruler or tape measure has centimetres and inches on it, you can read whichever measurement you wish.

Knitting is a hobby that I know you are going to enjoy. I wish you many happy hours of knitting.

Judith Dine

ACKNOWLEDGMENTS

Special thanks to Christine Hyde for her interest and assistance in checking the designs and manuscript.

All the yarns recommended in this book are produced by: R. V. Marriner Ltd., Keighley, Yorks.

The yarns are machine washable and are currently available through the normal retail outlets.

Abbreviations

The following abbreviations are used throughout

K	– knit	cm	– centimetre(s)
P	– purl	in(s)	– inch(es)
st(s)	– stitch(es)	patt.	– pattern
g st	– garter stitch	sl	– slip
m st	– moss stitch	psso.	– pass slipped stitch over
st st	– stocking stitch	rep.	– repeat(ing)
alt.	– alternate (every 2nd row)	tog.	– together
beg.	– begin(ning)	YF	– yarn forward
MC	– main colour	YB	– yarn back
CC	– contrast colour	YRN	– yarn round needle
FC	– first colour	rem.	– remain(ing)
SC	– second colour	tbl	– through back of loop(s)
LC	– light colour	YON	– yarn over needle
DC	– dark colour	No	– number
cont.	– continue	g	– gram
dec.	– decrease	approx	– approximately
inc.	– increase	foll.	– following

Additional abbreviations are given at the beginning of the instructions for certain patterns.
The asterisk (*) is used in a pattern as a form of repetition. Figures stated after the asterisk are to be repeated as many times as stated in the instructions. For example: *K6, P1, repeat from * twice, will be worked by knitting 6 stitches, purling 1 stitch, then knitting 6 stitches, purling 1, knitting 6, purling 1. This means that when you have worked the first 7 stitches, you work 7 more stitches twice, so there will be 21 stitches worked altogether..

Helpful Hints

- Don't rush your work. Work slowly and be patient.
- Wash your hands before you begin to knit. Dirty hands will make your yarn 'fluff' and leave marks on your work.
- Remember that tension is most important in knitting.
- Keep making small items until you feel you are able to cope with the many hours it will take you to make a larger item.
- Don't cast off tightly. Use a size larger needle if necessary.
- Wash your knitting needles from time to time as, like everything else, they gather dirt.
- Don't use needles that are too long for your work. When knitting small items choose the shortest needles possible for the job.
- Wash knitted items before they get too dirty. Use a gentle washing powder or liquid detergent—never soap.
- Always use the yarn listed for the particular item you are going to make.
- Knit evenly and check tension often.
- Take your time when making up as a badly made up item will never look good.
- When not in use, wrap your knitting in a clean cloth or keep it in a knitting bag.
- Don't leave your knitting in the middle of a row, always work to the end before leaving it aside.
- When your pattern tells you to buy a certain amount of yarn to make the design, buy all the yarn at the one time. Dye-lots vary, which means that one packet of yarn could be a slightly different colour from the next packet of the same colour yarn opened.
- Don't let anyone 'help you with a few rows'. No two people knit alike.
- Before you begin any pattern read through the instructions first, and if you don't understand anything, ask an experienced knitter.
- Don't split stitches by putting the needle through the yarn instead of through the stitch.
- Use a clearly marked tape or ruler to measure your work. Always measure your work on a flat surface (table, floor, etc.).
- If you have left your knitting aside for a time, the stitches on the needle will have stretched, so unpick the row last worked before you begin again.
- When you have trouble with your work don't keep on trying, but leave it aside and come back to it when your mind is fresh again.

Equipment

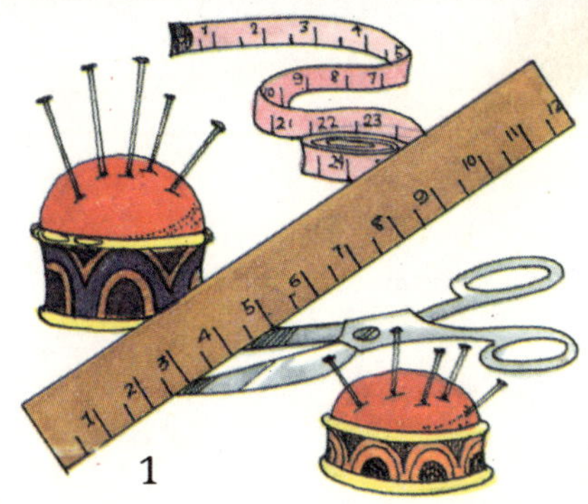
1

All you need to begin with are needles and yarn, but as you learn more about knitting and start to follow patterns you will need the following:
Tape Measure or Ruler (1)
Scissors (1)
Pins (1)
Tapestry Needle (a large-eyed blunt needle used in making up (2)
Stitch Holder (used when stitches are left aside) (3)
Crochet Hook (used for picking up any dropped stitches) (4)
Cable Needle (a small double-pointed needle used in cable patterns) (5)
Clean Cloth or Knitting Bag (as container for work when not in use) (6)

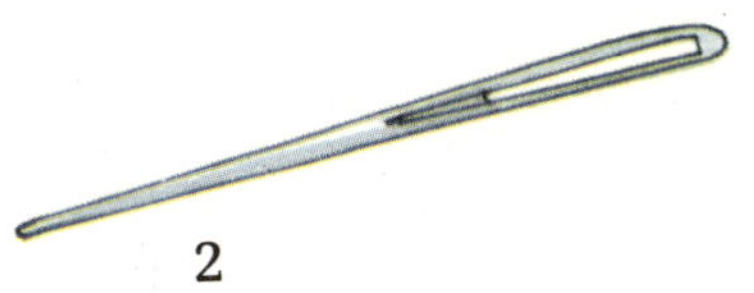
2

YARN

Yarn is a word we use to describe all knitting threads – wool, mohair, synthetics and wool-and-synthetic mixtures.

PLY

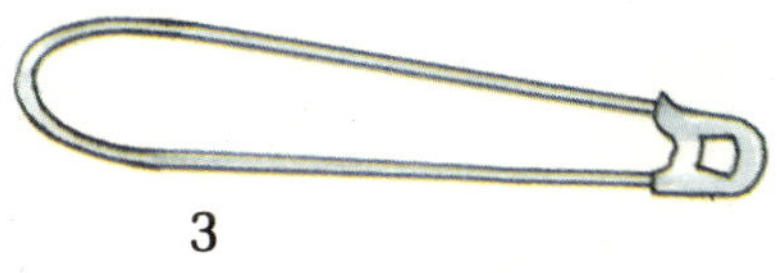
3

Yarn is thin or thick according to the ply – 3-ply is three lengths of yarn stranded together, 4-ply is four lengths of yarn stranded together and so on. A manufacturer can make these lengths of yarn as thin or as thick as he wishes, therefore not all yarns of the same ply are the same thickness. Always use the yarn listed for the pattern you intend to make.

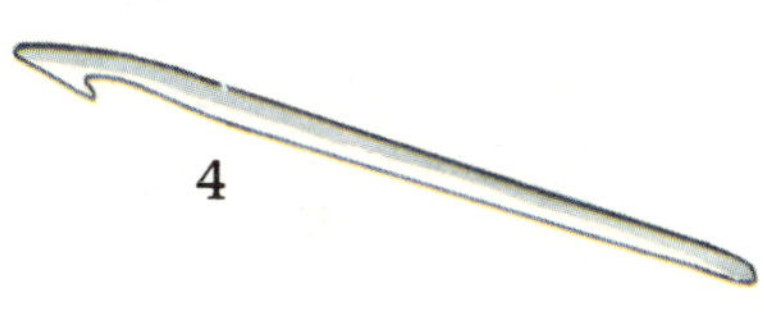
4

NEEDLES

Standard knitting needles (7) are made in various sizes and lengths. Use 'Aero' needles as often as you can because they are made of strong alloy metal and cannot break. If you use bone or plastic needles make sure you have a contrast colour to the yarn you intend to use. For example, if your yarn is blue, choose red needles not blue needles or your eyes will strain trying to see the stitches.
Double-pointed needles (8) are always sold in sets of four in various sizes and are used for knitting neckbands, socks, gloves, etc. When using double-pointed needles you are knitting in a circular (around-and-around) style and will not have any seams.
Circular needles (9) are sold in various sizes and lengths and are used in a similar way to double-pointed needles, but usually for larger items such as skirts and sweaters.

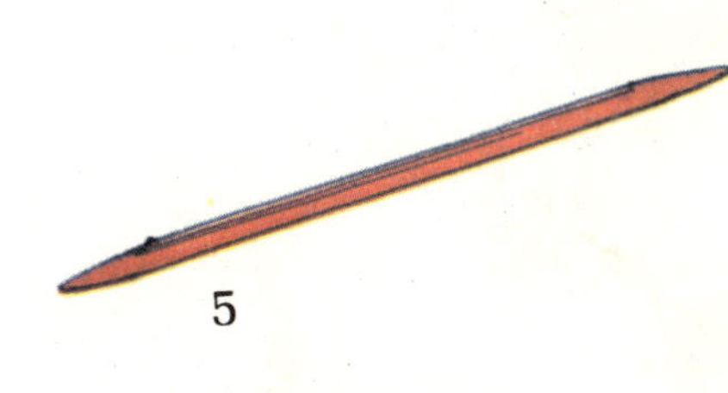
5

6

7

Learning to Knit

CASTING ON

Putting the first row of stitches on the needle is called casting on. Begin with a SLIP LOOP which will form the first stitch.

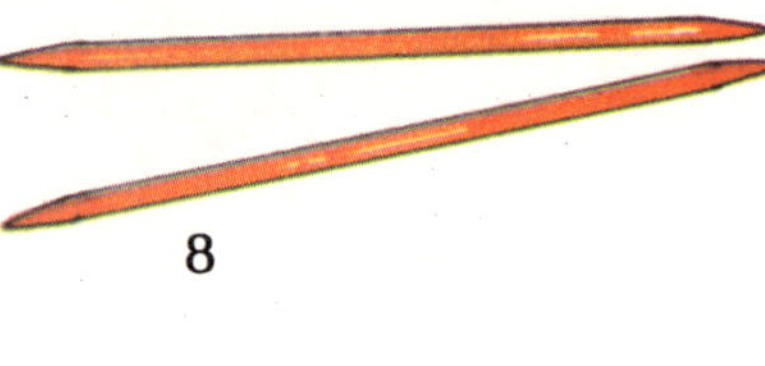
8

- Hold the yarn between your left forefinger and thumb. Take the yarn in your right hand and make a loop around the first two fingers of your left hand, then hold the loop with your left thumb. (10)
- Slip a needle through the loop, then draw a length of yarn through the loop. (11)
- Pull firmly on the yarn ends. (12)

Now that you have the slip loop firmly on the needle you are ready to cast on by one of the following two methods:

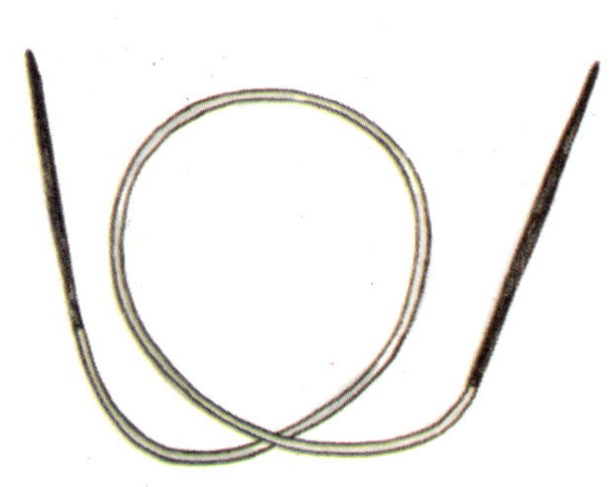
9

THE THUMB METHOD (USING ONE NEEDLE)

- Undo a long piece of yarn (about one yard). Make a slip loop on the needle. With the short length of yarn in the left hand pass this around the left-hand thumb. (13)
- Put the point of the needle beneath the loop on the thumb and draw the loop up firmly. Then, holding the yarn from the ball in the right hand, pass it around the point of the needle and draw it through the loop on the thumb. Pull the yarn to tighten the stitch. (14)

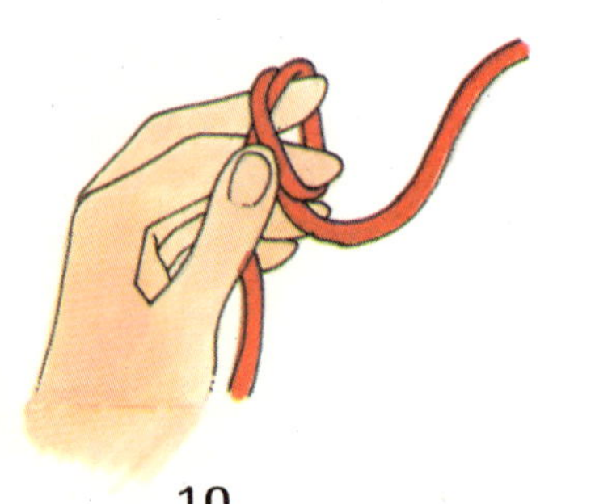
10

Continue until you have enough stitches on your needle.

THE TWO-NEEDLE METHOD

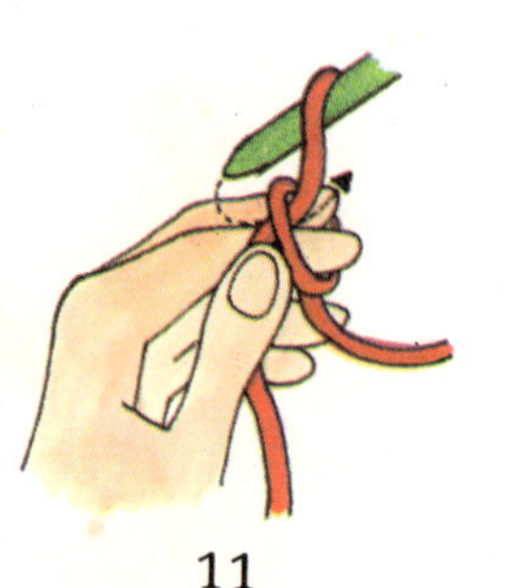
11

- Make a slip loop on the needle at least 7.5 centimetres (3 inches) from the end of the yarn, then put the needle in your left hand. Put the point of the right-hand needle through the stitch from front to back of stitch, then bring the yarn from the back between the needles and over the right-hand needle. With the right-hand needle draw the yarn through the loop to make a stitch, then put the stitch on the left-hand needle. (15)
- You now have two stitches on the left-hand needle. Put the right-hand needle between the two stitches and make a stitch. (16)

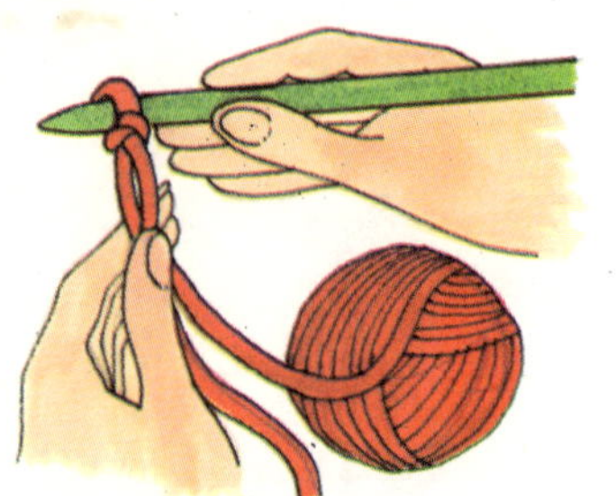
12

Continue until you have enough stitches on your needle.

BASIC STITCHES

Now that you have cast on, you are ready to start work. There are only two basic stitches used in knitting: the knit stitch (sometimes called plain) and the purl stitch. Every fancy pattern is made up of these two basic stitches worked in different ways.

13

THE KNIT STITCH

This stitch is shown in pattern instructions as **K**.

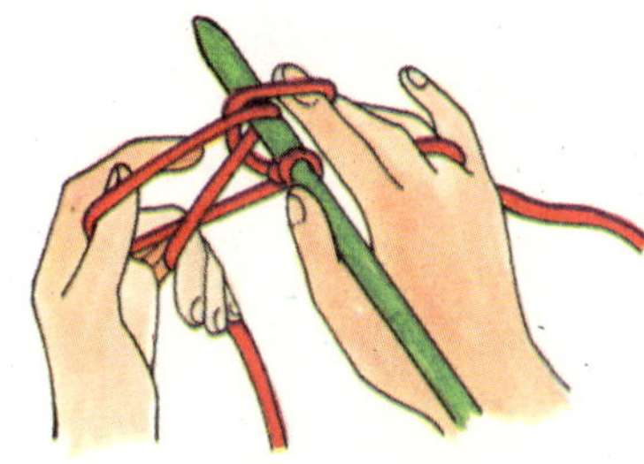

14

- With the yarn at back of work put the point of the right-hand needle IN through the first stitch on the left-hand needle from front to back, then, while holding the yarn in the right hand, pass the yarn OVER the point of the right-hand needle. (17)
- Bring the loop THROUGH the stitch on the left-hand needle with the point of the right-hand needle. Slip the stitch OFF the left-hand needle. (18)

Keep saying to yourself IN-OVER-THROUGH-OFF.

15

THE PURL STITCH

This stitch is shown in pattern instructions as **P**.

- With the yarn at front of work put the point of the right-hand needle IN through the first stitch on the left-hand needle from back to front, then pass the yarn OVER the point of the right-hand needle. (19).
- Bring the loop THROUGH the stitch on the left-hand needle. Slip the stitch OFF the needle. (20)

16

Keep saying to yourself IN-OVER-THROUGH-OFF.

17

CASTING OFF

When you want to end your work you simply cast off so as to make a firm edge that you cannot pull undone.

18

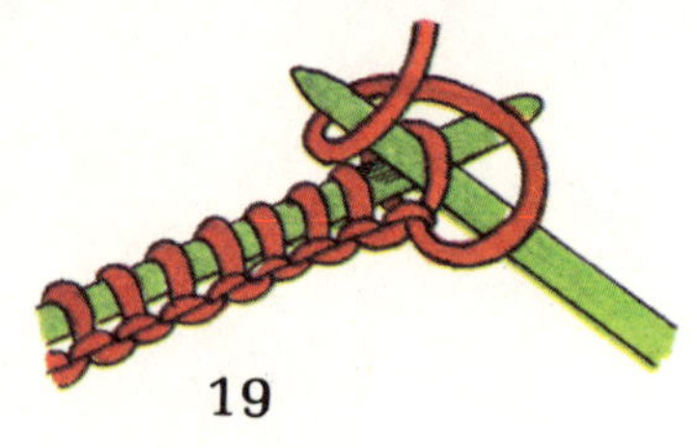
19

- Knit the first two stitches on the left-hand needle on to the right-hand needle, then place the point of the left-hand needle under the first stitch on the right-hand needle and lift it over the second stitch. Drop this stitch off the needle, knit the next stitch and then continue along the row lifting one stitch over the next until only one loop remains. (21)
- Cut the yarn and bring the end through the last stitch. During making up you will sew this end in to the work. (22)

20

When a pattern tells you to 'cast off ribwise' or to 'cast off in pattern', simply work in the same stitch casting off by lifting the second stitch on the right-hand needle over the first stitch as you would in the usual way.

TENSION

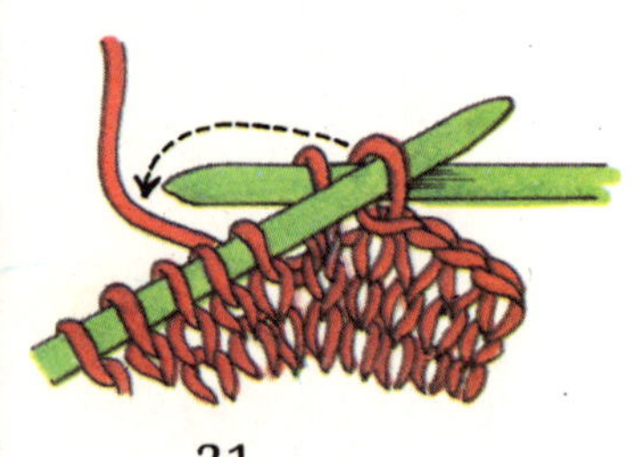
21

You will notice that all instructions give a 'Tension', usually placed underneath the 'Materials' section. Tension simply means the number of stitches the designer worked to the centimetre(s) or inch(es) when the original design was made.

How to check tension: Cast on enough stitches to measure 10.2 centimetres (4 inches) in width, using the yarn and needles you are going to use in your pattern. Work about 10.2 centimetres (4 inches) in the stitch given in your instructions, then cast off. Place the piece on a flat surface and measure with a ruler or tape measure the tension given (maybe 7sts to the centimetre or inch, or 7½sts to 5 centimetres or 2 inches). Put a pin either side of the tension measurement, then measure again to see if you have the tension. (23) If you have more stitches to the centimetre or inch, make another piece using larger sized needles; if you have fewer stitches, use smaller sized needles. Don't go on until the tension is right. Practise and practise until you understand what tension is all about, because good tension means good knitting—and correct fit.

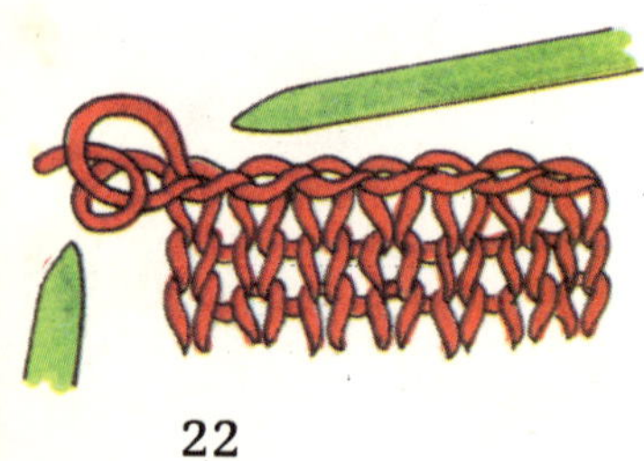
22

SHAPING

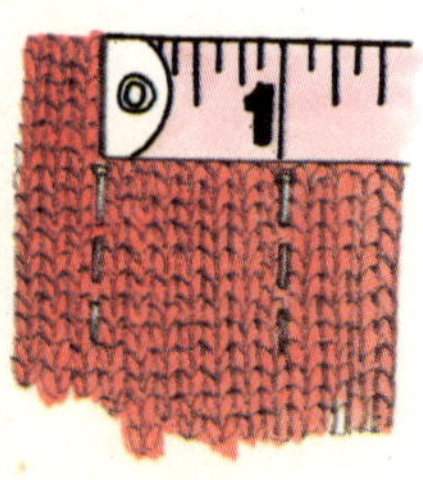

23

You will soon find that knitting a straight piece is easy. Then you will want to follow a pattern that is 'shaped' by way of increasing and decreasing:

INCREASING (MAKE EXTRA STITCHES)

At the beginning or end of a row, knit or purl the stitch in the ordinary way but don't drop the stitch off the needle. Put the point of the right-hand needle into the back of the stitch and knit or purl into the stitch again so that two stitches have been made. This method is used for side shapings. Another way of increasing is by picking up a loop lying between the needles, placing it on the left-hand needle, and knitting into the back of it. This method is used in the middle of a row. (24)

24

Increasing by bringing yarn forward (YF)
This method is used in fancy patterns between two knit stitches. Simply bring the yarn forward and then over the needle to begin working the next stitch. (25)

25

Increasing by taking yarn round needle (YRN)
This method is used in fancy patterns between two purl stitches. Bring the yarn around and over the needle to form a stitch without knitting it. (26)

26

Increasing by taking yarn over needle (YON)
This method is used between purl and knit stitches. Simply bring the yarn over the needle to begin the knit stitch. (27)

DECREASING (LOSING STITCHES)

The easiest way of decreasing is by knitting two stitches together to form one stitch. (28)

27

Two stitches can be purled together in the same way.

Decreasing by slipping a stitch (sl 1), knitting next stitch (K1), then passing slip stitch over the K1 (psso).

- Slip next stitch on to right-hand needle without working it. (29)

28

- Knit next st, then pass the slipped stitch over the knitted stitch by using the point of the left-hand needle in the same way as casting off. (30)

Decreasing by knitting through back of stitches (tbl).

Knitting 2 stitches together tbl is simply a form of decreasing by 'twisting' the stitch. Knit two stitches together in the usual way to form one stitch, but work through the back loops instead of the front loops.

29

JOINING IN NEW YARN

When you have to join in a new ball of yarn do so at the beginning of a row, leaving about 7·5 centimetres (3 inches) hanging at the end to darn into the work when you are making-up. (31) NEVER join in a new ball in the middle of a row.

30

GRAFTING

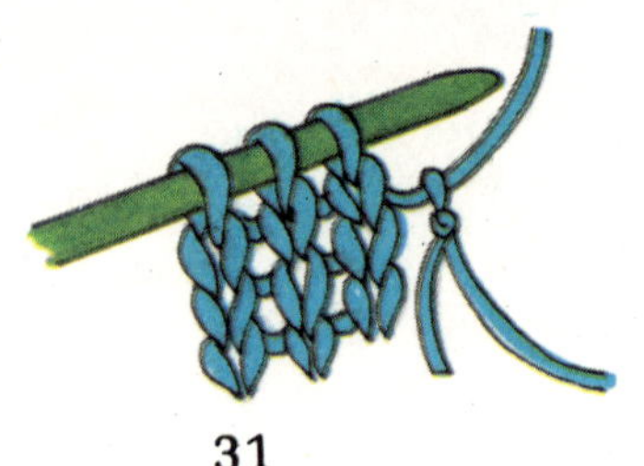
31

When you want to join two separate sets of stitches together (in the case of mittens, socks, etc.) without making a seam, you simply graft the stitches together.

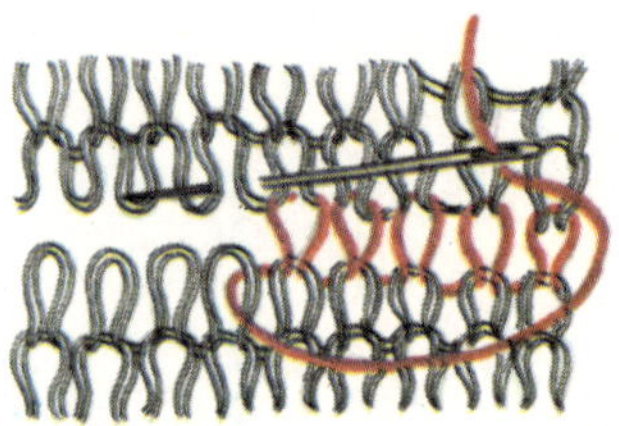
32

Firstly, you must have the same number of stitches on each of the needles facing each other (wrong sides of work facing each other) then, with a tapestry needle and the same yarn as you have been working with, proceed as follows: * Put the needle through the back stitch as if to knit, then through the front stitch as if to purl, leaving the stitches on the knitting needles. Put the needle through the back stitch as if to purl and drop the stitch off the knitting needle, put the needle through the next stitch on the back needle as if to knit and leave the knitted stitch on the knitting needle. Put the needle through the front stitch as if to knit and drop the stitch off the knitting needle, put the needle through the next stitch on the front needle as if to purl and leave the knitted stitch on the knitting needle*; repeat from * to * until all the stitches have been joined together. (32)

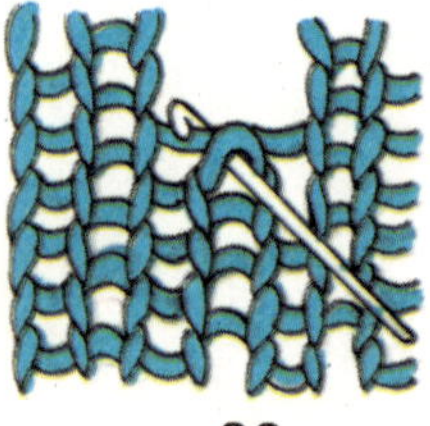
33

PICKING UP DROPPED STITCHES

Every knitter makes mistakes. Fortunately it is very easy to pick up a dropped stitch. With the right side of the work facing you, use a crochet hook to pick up the stitch and work it through each loop until you reach the row you are working. (33)

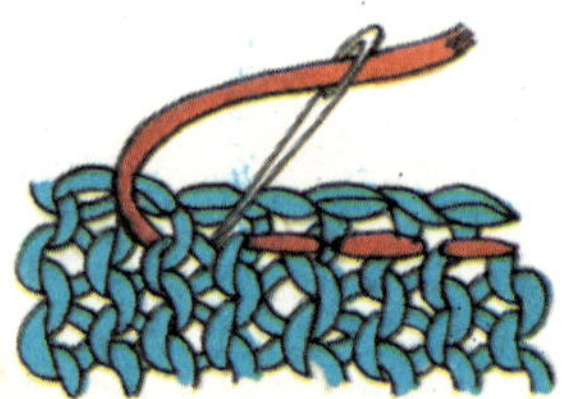
34

MAKING UP

Using a tapestry needle, darn in all ends.

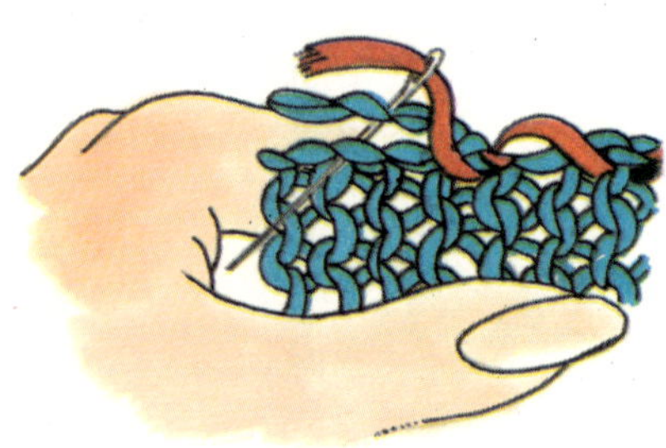
35

PRESSING

Wool: Press lightly on the wrong side with a steam iron, or with a warm iron over a damp cloth.
Synthetics: Do not press.

SEAMING

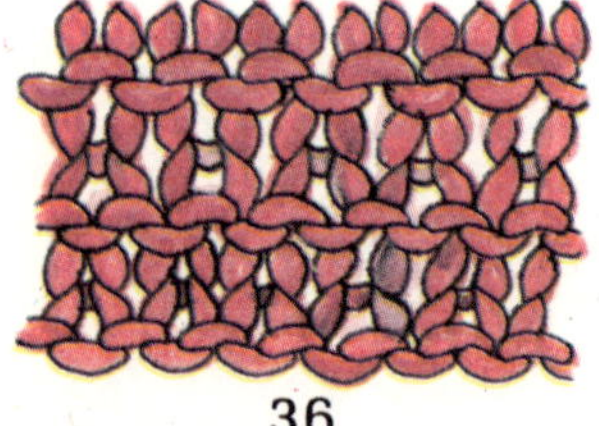
36

Pin pieces together, right sides of work facing, being careful not to stretch the knitting.

There are only two seams used in making up; use a tapestry needle and the same yarn as your knitted item:

THE BACKSTITCH SEAM

37

Sew the pieces together one stitch in from the edge as shown in diagram, with right sides facing each other. (34)

THE FLAT SEAM

Oversew pieces together along edge, with wrong sides of work facing you. (35)

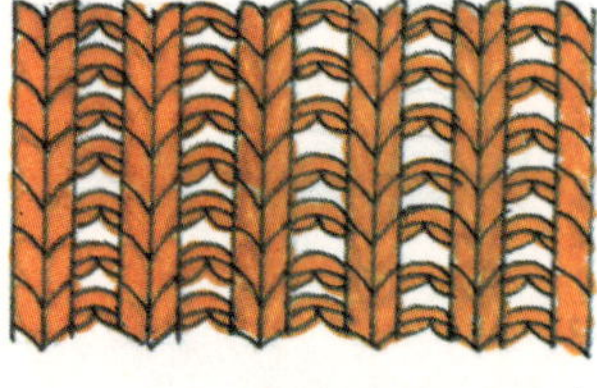

38

STITCH PATTERNS

GARTER STITCH

Garter stitch is shown as **g st** in the abbreviations and is worked by knitting every row, which gives a series of 'ridges'. It takes two rows to form one ridge. There is no right or wrong side to garter stitch. (36)

39

STOCKING STITCH

This stitch is shown as **st st** in the abbreviations and is made by knitting one row then purling the second row. The knit side is the right side of work. (37)

REVERSED STOCKING STITCH

40

The wrong side, or the purl side, of stocking stitch is often used as a pattern and is called reversed stocking stitch.

RIBBING

The most popular rib stitch is the K1, P1 rib which is often used for neckbands, basques, belts, cuffs, etc., and is simple to do:
Cast on an even number of stitches.
Rib row: * K1, P1; repeat from * to end of row. Repeat above row for length required. (38)

41

Another popular rib stitch is the K2, P2 rib:
Cast on a number of stitches divisible by 4.
Rib row: * K2, P2; repeat from * to end of row. Repeat above row for length required. (39)

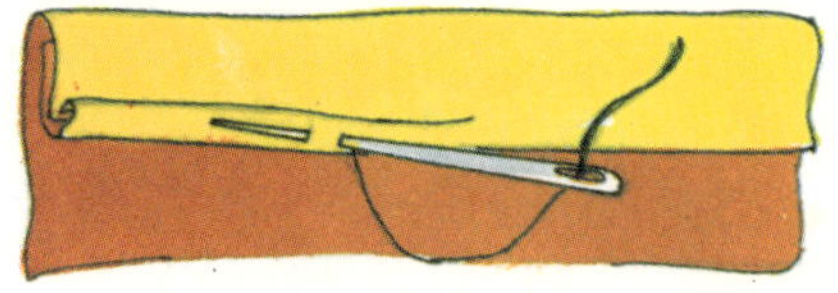

42

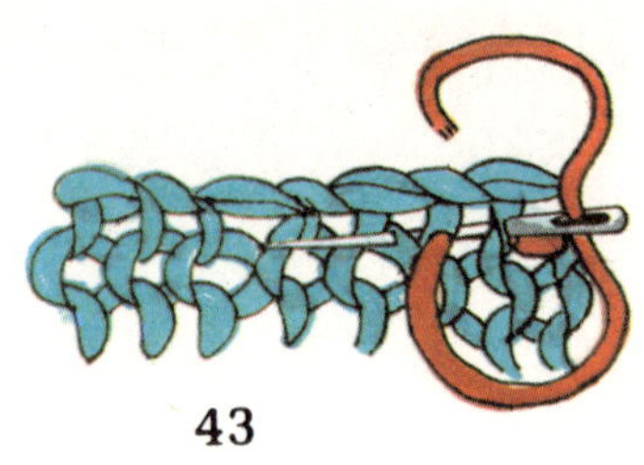

43

MOSS STITCH

This stitch is shown as **m st** in the abbreviations and is a very popular and easy stitch:
Cast on an uneven number of stitches.
M st row: K1, * P1, K1; repeat from * to end of row. Repeat above row for length required.
There is no right or wrong side to moss stitch. (40)

CABLE

Cable patterns are easy to do when you know how! The finished look is like a twisted rope effect. Here is an easy cable stitch for you to start practising:
Cast on a multiple of 9, plus 5 (say 23sts).
1st row: Sl 1, * P3, K6; repeat from * to last 4sts, P3, K1.
2nd row: Sl 1, * K3, P6; repeat from * to last 4sts, K4.
Rep. above 2 rows once more.
5th row: Sl 1, * P3, sl next 3sts on a cable needle and hold at back of work, K3 sts from left-hand needle, K3 sts from cable needle (called c 3f), repeat from * to last 4sts, P3, K1.
6th row: As 2nd row.
Repeat 1st and 2nd rows 3 times more.
13th row: Sl 1, * P3, sl next 3sts on to cable needle, and hold at front of work, K3 sts from left-hand needle, K3 sts from cable needle (called c 3f); repeat from * to last 4sts, P3, K1.
14th row: As 2nd row.
Repeat 1st and 2nd rows once more.
Repeat above 16 rows. (41)

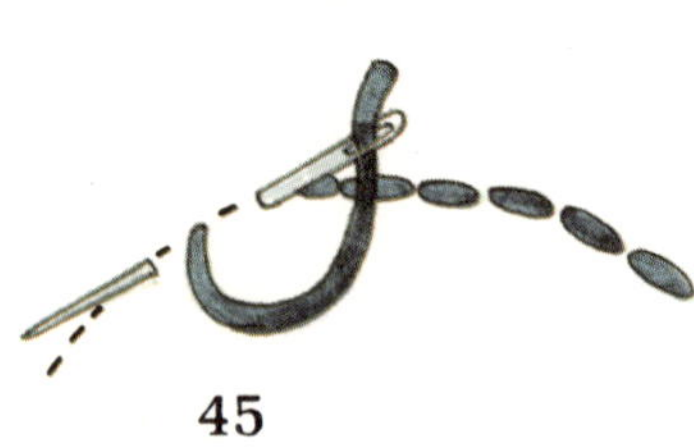

44

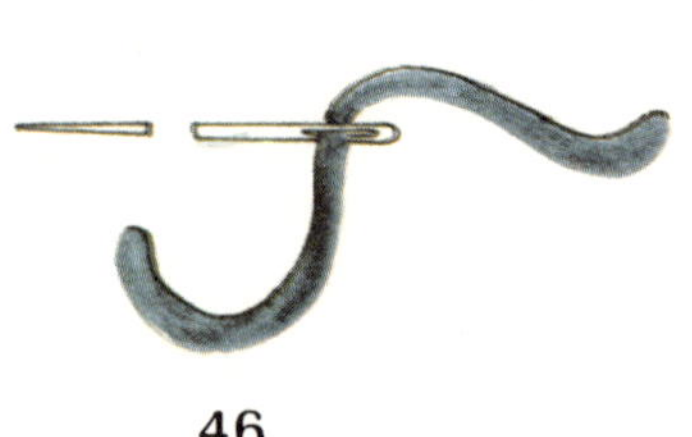

45

SEWING STITCHES YOU WILL NEED TO KNOW

SLIP STITCH

The slip stitch is used when stitching should not show. It is a tiny hand-stitch taken through and under a fold of fabric. Place a stitch through the fold of fabric about .3 to .6 centimetre ($\frac{1}{8}$ to $\frac{1}{4}$ inch) in length. Pick up only one or two threads of the under fabric. Continue in this way, taking a stitch through the fold and then in the under fabric, until you have completed the work. (42)

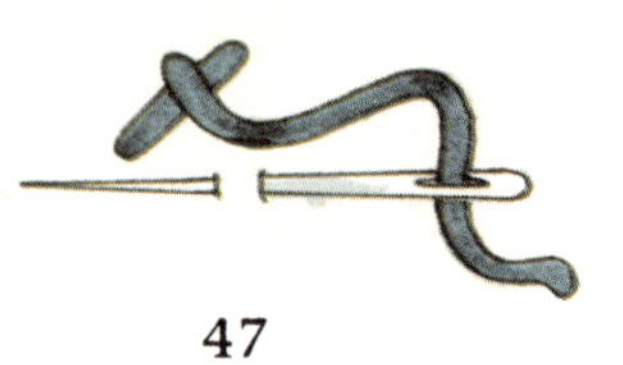

46

BACKSTITCH

Backstitch is placed end to end at the front of the fabric. This creates a double thread at the back. It is an ideal solid border line or strong seam. For most work the stitch should be short.

1. Pin along the sides to be backstitch seamed, taking care to match the fabric row by row throughout. Work from right to left. Make a small stitch like a tacking stitch and then insert the needle point about .6 centimetre ($\frac{1}{4}$ inch) further along the seam. Draw the needle through the pieces of fabric. * (43)
2. Insert the needle point into the end of the last stitch and bring it forward and out .6 centimetre ($\frac{1}{4}$ inch) further along the pinned seam. Repeat from * until the seam is completed. (44)
   Note: To make your work neater insert the needle into the same place as the end of the last stitch. (45)

47

48

HERRINGBONE STITCH

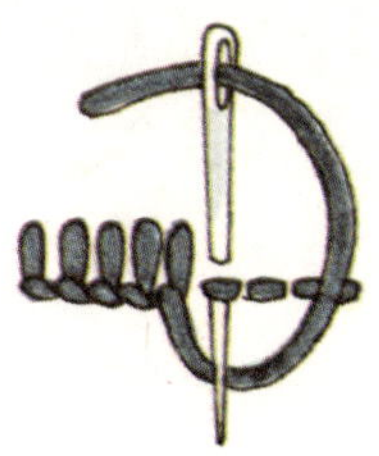
49

This pretty stitch with a lattice appearance is useful for making flat borders in embroidery and for sewing down a hem on thick material. If you are making a bulky garment you need to make a single hem turning only, then pin and tack down the raw edge and, using the herringbone stitch, sew the hem flat to the material.

1. Start at lower left and work from left to right. Bring the needle out through the fabric, and make a long stitch on a slant to the right. Insert needle and make a short stitch to the left. (46)
2. Carry needle downwards over the first long stitch to the right and insert it through the fabric. (47) Make a short stitch to the left. Repeat from beginning. (48)

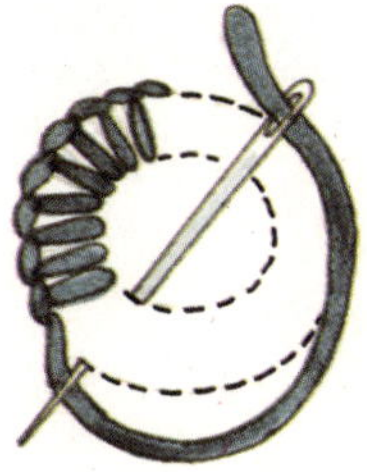
50

BUTTONHOLE STITCH

This stitch has many uses. It can be used as an outline, as a border on necklines, or to make a sturdy buttonhole. (49, 50)

1. To start, make a straight upright stitch the width of the outline to be covered. Put the needle through to the wrong side at the end of this stitch, bringing it up again on the outline, where it first came through.
2. Make a second upright stitch, this time downwards, .6 centimetre ($\frac{1}{4}$ inch) from the first. Be sure to hold the thread down with your left thumb so that it is under the needle. Pull up the thread, and it will form a bar along the edge of the outline, known as the purl. Every type of buttonhole stitch has this purl.
3. Keep making upright stitches .6 centimetre ($\frac{1}{4}$ inch) apart, always keeping the thread under the needle.

51

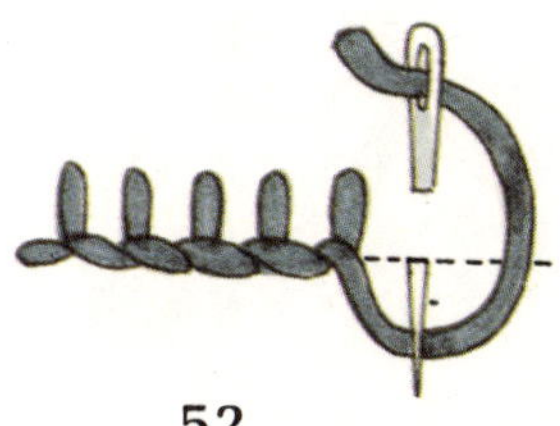
52

BLANKET STITCH

Work from right to left with your thread at the bottom edge.

1. Point the needle downwards, push it through the material from front to back, and bring it out between the material and the thread. (51)
2. Pull the thread through and start again. Work all the stitches in the same way. (52)

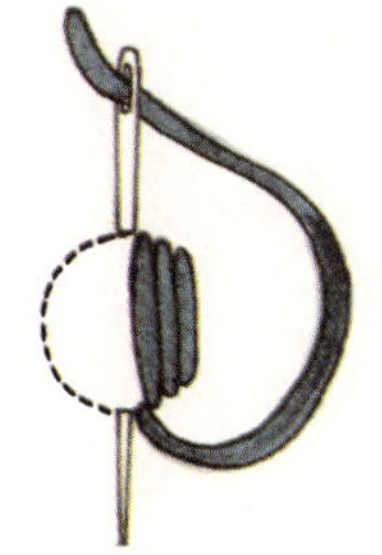
53

SATIN STITCH

Satin stitch is made up of a series of closely spaced long stitches lying side by side so closely that none of the fabric shows between them. The stitches go over and over, and are very close together. They can be straight up and down or slanted.

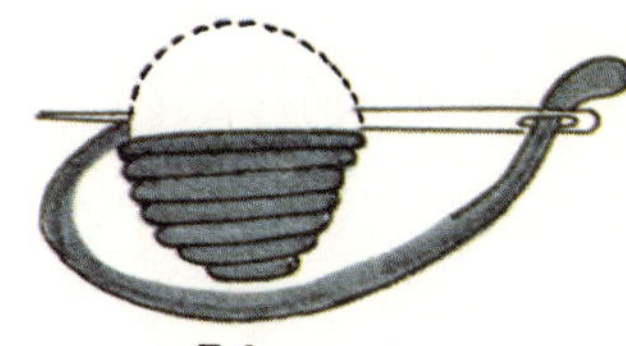
54

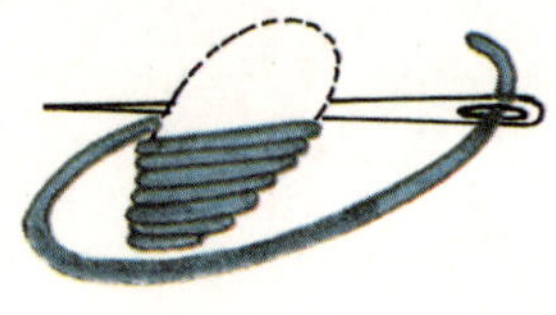

55

To work, bring the needle through to the right side on one edge of the outline to be filled, and put it in again exactly opposite on the other edge of the outline, making a straight line of thread across the space. Bring the needle up again as close as possible to the start of the first stitch, put it in again beside the end of the first stitch, and so on until the space is filled. (53, 54, 55)

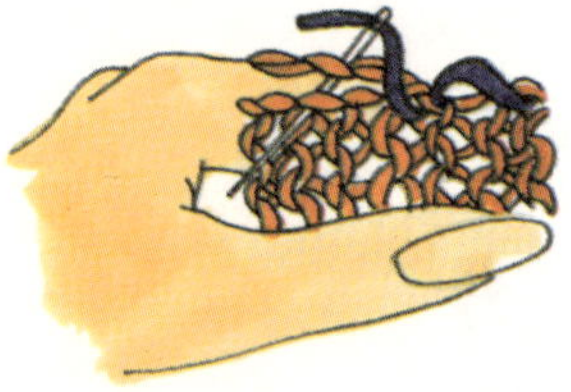

56

HOW TO MAKE A FLAT SEAM

With the right sides of your work facing, place the 2 pieces of work together, edge to edge. Place the forefinger of your left hand just between these edges. Using an overcasting stitch draw the edges together over your finger. Move your finger along as you work. (56)

57

HOW TO SEW ON A BUTTON

Place the button in its right position. Push your sewing needle up through the first hole, across and down through the second. Do this again for the third and fourth holes. Leave about .3 centimetre ($\frac{1}{8}$ inch) of thread (stem) between button and garment. Do this four times. (57)

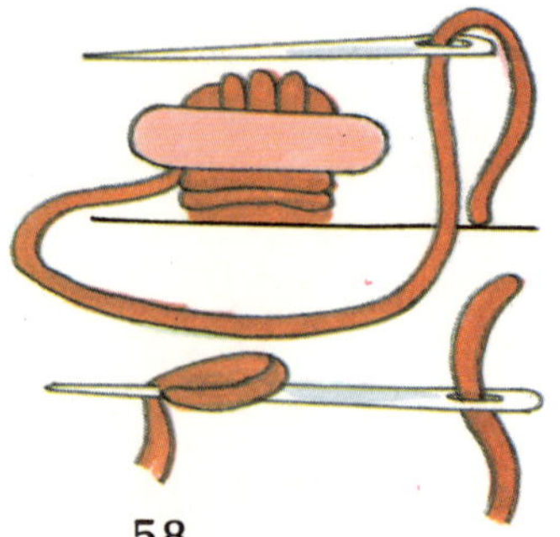

58

Wind the thread around the stem remaining between button and garment, and finish off with three backstitches on the wrong side. (58)

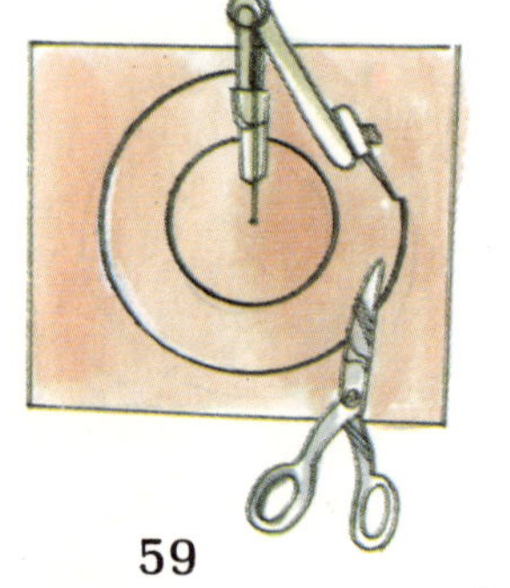

59

HOW TO MAKE A POMPON

Cut 2 circles of cardboard the size you require the pompon to be and cut out a circular hole in the centre of each – the larger the hole the thicker the pompon. (59) Wind yarn evenly around the 2 pieces of cardboard and through the centre hole until the hole is filled and you have to put the last strand through with a tapestry needle. (60) Break yarn. Cut through the yarn at the outer edge of the cardboard only. (61) Then tightly tie a piece of yarn around the cut pieces between the two circles of cardboard and, when strands are secured, cut away the cardboard and leave a length of yarn for sewing. Shake well and trim with scissors to neaten. (62)

60

HOW TO READ A KNITTING PATTERN

The knitting pattern is written in what is known as a knitter's code. Many knitting terms used in writing the pattern repeat themselves so often that a form of abbreviation is used for the repetition. At the beginning of this section a list of abbreviations with their full meanings is given for the knitting pattern instructions.

Patterns are set out in a certain form. At the beginning of the pattern, the section YOU WILL NEED (sometimes called MATERIALS) contains the brand of wool, the amount of wool in grams needed to knit the item, and the size of the needles it should be worked on.

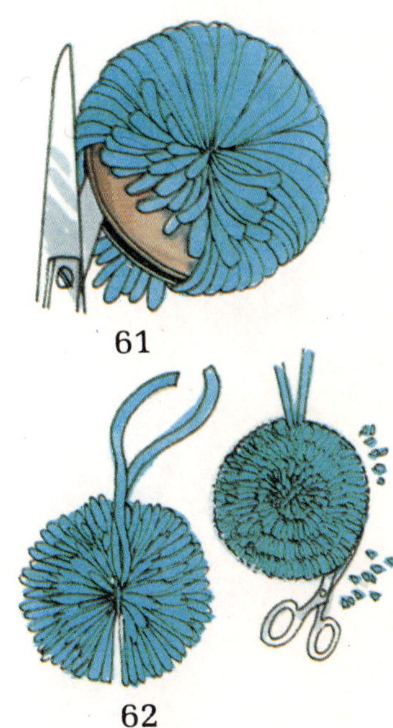
61

62

The next heading will be MEASUREMENTS. Here will appear the size of the finished knitted item.

TENSION will appear next. This is most important and a tension check must be made before you start to knit the pattern.

Next you will find the SPECIAL ABBREVIATIONS needed for that particular pattern. Make sure you fully understand their meaning. The usual abbreviations are listed under a main heading ABBREVIATIONS at the front of this section. Always read them through before you start to knit from the instructions and make sure you know just what they mean.

Finally you come to the INSTRUCTIONS, which is where you begin to knit. Read these instructions carefully, and follow them step by step in the order given.
For example, * K8, P3, repeat from * twice.
Knit 8 stitches, purl 3 stitches, then knit 8 stitches, purl 3, knit 8, purl 3. This means that having worked the first 11 stitches, you then work 11 more stitches twice. Altogether you will have worked 33 stitches.

The ASTERISK (*) means to repeat the section given from the * the number of times directed. For example, if your pattern says K1, * K2, P1; repeat from * 5 times, you really work the K2, P1 section 6 times altogether.

BRACKETS ( ) are given to separate the sizes. For example, if your instructions are written in 3 sizes such as 66 (71, 76) centimetre/26 (28, 30) inch chest and you wish to knit the third size: 76 centimetre (30 inch) chest, you simply follow the instructions for the third size throughout. It is a good idea to read through your instructions before you begin and draw a circle around the figures which apply to the size you will be knitting. Brackets are also used where a section of the pattern is to be repeated. For example, your instructions might tell you to 'K2, (P6, K4) to end', which means that you repeat the bracketed figures to the end of the row.

Under the heading TO MAKE UP you will find details of how to press and seam the knitted pieces, and how to join the seams to form the item.

Oven Mitt

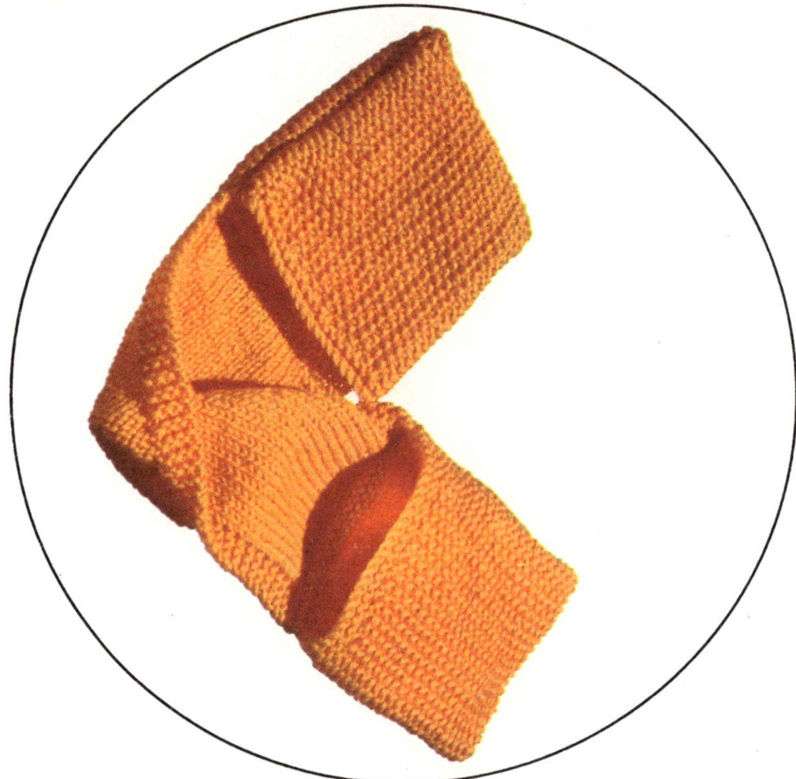

you will need

3 balls 40g Marriner Bouquet Chunky
Approx. 60% Courtelle 40% Nylon (machine washable).
Pair No 6 Aero Needles
Felt

measurements

66cm (26ins) long x 14cm ($5\frac{1}{2}$ins) wide.

tension

18sts and 21 rows to 10.2cm (4ins) over stocking stitch (st st)

instructions

With needles cast on 21sts.
1st row: (right side) K.
Rep. last row twice.
4th row: K3 sts, (K1, P1) rep. to last 4sts, K4.
Rep. last row until work measures 33cm (13ins) ending on a wrong side row.
K 4 rows.
Next row: K4, P to last 4sts, K4.
Next row: K.
Rep. last 2 rows until work measures 66cm (26ins) ending on a K row.
K 3 rows.
Next row: K3, (K1, P1) rep. to last 4sts, K4.
Rep. last row until work measures 99cm (39ins) ending on a right side row.
K 3 rows then cast off on next row.

To make up:
Press on the wrong side with a WARM iron and a DRY cloth. Fold moss stitch section in half (for mitts). Cut felt to fit mitt. With a slip stitch (see page 18) sew felt to inside of mitt. With right sides facing and using a small backstitch (see page 18) sew sides together leaving an opening for hands.

Tea Cosy

you will need

Marriner Aristocrat Superwash Double Knitting Pure New Wool (machine washable).
–2 balls 25g Light Colour (LC)
–2 balls 25g Dark Colour (DC)
Pair No 9 Aero Needles.

measurements

To fit 6-cup teapot

tension

12sts and 26 rows to 5.1cm (2ins).

instructions

(Make 2 pieces.) Beg. at lower edge with needles and LC cast on 'thumb' method 58sts.
1st row: (wrong side) K.
2nd row: P.
* 3rd row: K.
4th row: With DC, (K2, sl 2 purlwise) rep. to last 2sts, K2
5th row: (P2, sl 2 purlwise) rep. to last 2sts, P2.
6th row: As 4th row.
7th row: As 5th row.
8th row: With LC knit *.
Rep. these 8 rows 9 times.
Next row: As 1st row.
Eyelet row: P1, (P2 tog., YRN) rep. to last stitch, P1.
Work from * to * once.
K 1 row, then cast off on next row.

To make up:
Press on wrong side. With right sides of pieces facing and using a small backstitch (see page 18) sew sides, leaving an opening of 7.5cm (3ins) on each side for handle and spout. Press seams open.

To finish off:
With 4 strands of yarn make a twisted cord 81cm (32ins) long, thread through eyelets and tie in a bow.

Desmond Dog

you will need

Marriner Aristocrat Superwash Double Knitting Pure New Wool (machine washable)
–3 balls 25g Dark Colour (DC)
–2 balls 25g Light Colour (LC)
Pair No 9 Aero Needles
Ribbon
Felt for Eyes
Foam cushion filling
Small pieces of cardboard for pads

tension

23sts and 40 rows to 10.2cm (4ins) over garter stitch (g st)

instructions

BODY

With needles and DC cast on 5sts.
1st row: K.
2nd row: K1, inc. 1 stitch in each of the next 3sts, K1 (8sts).
3rd row: K.
4th row: K1, incl 1 stitch in each stitch to the last stitch, K1 (14sts).
Rep. the last 2 rows twice (50sts).
K 53 rows.
Next row: (K2 tog.) rep. to end (25sts).
Cast off on the next row.
Fold in half and join the side edges tog. leaving the other edge open and fill firmly. Draw up opening then fasten off.

HEAD

With needles and DC cast on 20sts and K 76 rows. Cast off on the next row. Fold work in half, having cast on edge facing cast off edge. Join the side edges and fill. Attach Head to Body.

MUZZLE

(2 pieces.) With needles and LC cast on 20sts and work in g st.
Knit 4 rows.
Next row: K and dec. 1 stitch each end (18sts).
Rep. the last 5 rows once (16sts).
Cast off on the next row. Join the 2 pieces tog. leaving the cast off edges open. Fill and attach the cast off edges in a circle to lower part of Head then sew into position.
Cut felt for Eyes and sew into place.

EARS

(2 pieces in each DC and LC.)
With needles cast on 8sts.
1st row: K.
2nd row: K and inc. 1 stitch each end (10sts).
Rep. the 1st and 2nd rows 6 times (22sts). K 9 rows.
Next row: K and dec. 1 stitch each end (20sts).
K 13 rows.
Next row: K and dec. 1 stitch each end (18sts).
Rep. the last row twice (14sts) then cast off on the next row.
Join tog. 1 piece of DC and 1 piece of LC leaving the cast off edges open.

Draw up the open ends and attach to Head.

PADS
(4.) With needles and LC cast on 5sts.
1st row: K.
2nd row: P and inc. 1 stitch each end (7sts).
3rd row: K and inc. 1 stitch each end (9sts).
4th row: As 2nd row (11 sts).
Cont. in st st. Work 6 rows straight then dec. 1 stitch each end of the next 3 rows (5sts). Cast off on the next row. Cut 4 pieces of cardboard slightly smaller than pads for inside base of pads.

FRONT LEGS
(2.) With needles and LC cast on 32sts and K 2 rows.
3rd row: K and inc. 1 stitch each end (34sts).
4th, 5th, 6th and 7th rows: K.
8th, 9th, 10th, 11th, 12th, 13th and 14th rows: K and dec. 1 stitch each end (20sts).
15th, 16th, 17th, 18th, 19th and 20th rows: K.
Break off LC and join DC.
21st, 22nd, 23rd, 24th, 25th and 26th rows: K.
27th row: * K and inc. 1 stitch each end.
K 14 rows *.
Rep. from * to * once (24sts).
Next row: K2 tog., K8, K2 tog., turn (leave rem. 12sts on holder).
Cont. on the 10sts and dec. 1 stitch each end of the next 4 rows (2sts).
Cast off on the next row. Join in yarn to the rem. 12sts and finish to correspond with other side.
Fold Legs in half and join the cast off edges tog. then join side edges.
Fill Legs then sew on pads with cardboard inserted inside round open ends.
Firmly sew Legs to Body.

BACK LEGS
(4 pieces.) With needles and DC cast on 9sts.
1st row: K.
2nd row: K and inc. 1 stitch each end (11 sts).
Rep. the 1st and 2nd rows 3 times (17sts).
9th and 10th rows: K.
11th row: K to the last stitch and inc. 1 stitch in last stitch.
K 18 rows.
30th row: K2 tog., K to end (17sts).
31st row: K.
Rep. the last 2 rows twice (15sts).
36th, 37th and 38th rows: K.
39th row: K to the last 2 sts, K2 tog. (14sts).
40th, 41st and 42nd rows: K.
43rd row: As 30th row.
44th row: As 39th row (12sts).
45th and 46th rows: K.
47th row: As 30th row.
48th row: K to the last stitch, inc. 1 stitch in last stitch (12sts).
49th and 50th rows: K.
51st and 52nd rows: K and dec. 1 stitch each end (8sts).
Cast off on the next row.
Sew each pr. of Legs tog. leaving an opening for filling.
Fill and sew up opening.

BACK FEET
(2.) With needles and LC cast on 32sts and K 2 rows.
3rd row: K and inc. 1 stitch each end (34sts).
4th, 5th, 6th and 7th rows: K.
8th, 9th, 10th, 11th, 12th, 13th and 14th rows: K and dec. 1 stitch each end (20sts).
15th row: K.
Cast off on the next row.
Fold in half and join edges tog.
Sew pads into place with cardboard inserted inside then fill.
Sew the open edge of Foot round the narrow end of Leg.
Attach Legs to Body.

TAIL
With needles and DC cast on 3sts and K 1 row. Inc. 1 stitch each end of every foll. row until 23sts. K 6 rows.
Next row: K and dec. 1 stitch each end (21sts).
Rep. the last 7 rows twice (17sts).
Break off DC and join LC.
Rep. the last 7 rows until 11sts rem. Dec. 1 stitch each end of every row until 3sts rem., then cast off on the next row. Fold in half lengthwise and join the side edges and pointed end.
Fill Tail and attach to Body.

Clarence Clown

you will need

Marriner Aristocrat Superwash Double Knitting Pure New Wool (machine washable)
–5 balls 25g Main Colour (MC)
–2 balls 25g First Colour (FC)
–1 ball 25g of 4 more Contrast Colours CC for Patched Pants.
Pair No 9 Aero Needles
Foam cushion filling
Felt

tension

24sts and 32 rows to 10.2cm (4ins)

abbreviation

Inc. 1st: Pick up horizontal loop before next st and knit tbl

instructions

FEET
(Make 2.) With MC and needles cast on 58sts and work 8 rows in st st.
9th row: K27, K2 tog., K2 tog. tbl, K to end (56sts).
10th row: P.
11th row: K26, K2 tog., K2 tog. tbl, K to end (54sts).
12th row: P to end, then sl last 27sts just worked back on to left needle, fold work in half, and with a 38cm (15in) length of yarn, graft first 12sts from each needle, sl rem. 15sts back on to right needle, then fasten off grafting yarn.
Work 4 rows on these 30sts then proceed for Leg as follows.

LEG
1st row: Work and inc. 1 stitch in every stitch to end (60sts).
Work 3 rows.
5th row: K14, * (inc. 1 stitch, K4) 3 times, inc. 1 stitch, K3, inc. 1 stitch in next st*, rep. from * to * once, K to end (70sts).
Work 1 row, then cast off on next row.

PANTS
With CC cast on 19sts and work 28 rows in moss stitch (m st) or until square has been completed then cast off in patt.
Work 23 more squares in the same way using the 6 colours and making 4 squares of each colour.
To Join Squares: With a flat seam join two sets of squares as follows: 4 squares wide and 3 squares long for each Leg (12 squares to each Leg). Fold each Leg in half and join the 3 squares tog. for each Leg. Fill Legs with foam pieces.

FRONT BODY
With MC and needles neatly pick up and knit 64sts across the front 4 squares (16sts on each square).
Next row: Work and evenly dec. 8sts on row (56sts).
Work in m st for 13cm (5ins).
Shape Shoulders: Cast off 5sts at beg. of the next 6 rows (26sts), then break yarn.
Join in FC and proceed for Head as follows.

HEAD
Beg. with a K row, cont. in stocking stitch (st st) at the same time dec. 1 stitch each end of the first row then work 3 rows straight. Inc. 1 stitch each end of next row then every row until 32sts rem. K1 row. Inc. 1 stitch each end of the next and every alternate row until 44sts ending on a P row. Cast on 5sts at beg. of the next 2 rows. Work 10 rows straight. Cast off 5 sts at beg. of the next 2 rows, then dec. 1 stitch each end of every row until 32sts rem. Cast off 6sts at beg. of the next 4 rows then cast off rem. 8sts.

BACK BODY
Work as Front Body across the back 4 squares. Join Body pieces for 7.5cm (3ins) then fill Body firmly.

ARMS
(Make 2.) Beg. at top, with MC cast on 2sts.
Work in m st and inc. 1 stitch each end of the next then every alternate row until 28sts. Cont. until Arms measure 13cm (5ins) from beg.
Next row: K1, inc. 1 stitch, work 11sts, (K2 tog.) twice, work 11sts, inc. 1 stitch, K1.
Work 2 rows. Rep. last 3 rows until Arms measure 16.5cm ($6\frac{1}{2}$ins.)
Next row: (K2 tog.) rep. to end.
P 1 row, change to FC and work 10 rows in st st.
Next row: K1, K2 tog., K3, K2 tog., K3, K2 tog., K1.
Next row: P.
Cast off on next row.
Sew up seams and fill Arms.
Sew up Shoulders and sew on Arms.

HAT
With MC and needles cast on 79sts and work in m st.
Work 2 rows.
3rd row: Work 2 tog., work 16sts, (work 2 tog.) twice, work 16sts, work 3 tog., work 16sts, (work 2 tog.) twice, work 16sts, work 2 tog. (71sts).
Work 3 rows straight.
7th row: Work 2 tog., work 14sts, (work 2 tog.) twice, work 14sts, work 3 tog., work 14sts, (work 2 tog.) twice, work 14sts, work 2 tog.
Work 3 rows straight. Cont. to dec. 8sts in this way on every foll. 4th row until 15sts rem.
Work 1 row.
Next row: Work and dec. 1 stitch at each end.
Next row: As last row.
Next row: K1, (work 3sts tog.) 3 times, K1 (5sts).
Next row: K2 tog., K1, K2 tog.
Next row: K3 tog., fasten off.

To make up:
Join feet seams and fill. With slip stitch sew feet to bottom of Pants, being careful to have toes facing forward. With a flat seam join the sides of Hat. Make a pompon and attach to top. Using small backstitch sew up sides of Neck leaving top of Head open. Fill all parts then sew Head opening. Sew on Hat. Cut features from Felt as illustrated. Using yarns left over from squares in Pants make Pompons (see page 20) and attach at centre Front of Top.

Gilbert Golliwog

you will need

Marriner Bouquet 4 Ply. Approx. 60% Courtelle 40% Nylon (machine washable).
–2 balls 20g 1st Colour (A)
–1 ball 20g 2nd Colour (B)
–1 ball 20g 3rd Colour (C)
Scraps of black, white and red felts for features
2 curtain rings
Foam cushion filling
Pair No 10 Aero Needles

measurements

Approximately 56cm (22ins) tall

tension

28sts and 36 rows to 10.2cm (4ins)

instructions

FRONT LEGS AND BODY
* With A cast on 15sts and work in garter stitch (g st) for 2 rows.
3rd row: K7, (K1, P1, K1) all into the next stitch, K7 (17sts).
4th row: K7, inc. 1 stitch in the next stitch, K1, inc. 1 stitch in the next stitch, K7 (19sts).
Cont. in this way inc. 2sts on every row until 29sts.
Break off A and join in C. K 2 rows.
Next row: K13, K3 tog., K13 (27sts).
Next row: K12, K3 tog., K12 (25sts).
Cont. to dec. in this way until 15sts rem. K 1 row.
** Break off C and join in A, K 60 rows. * Leave sts on holder.
Rep. from * to * for other Leg.
Next row: K15, cast on 3sts, K15 from holder (33sts).
Cont. on the last sts for Body and K 9 rows. Break off A, join in C and K 1 row.
Work in rib of K1, P1 for 6 rows.
Next row: Rib 3, (inc. 1, rib 4) rep.

to end (39sts).
Proceed in patt. as follows:
*** Join in B, K 2 rows.
3rd row: Join in C, K1, (sl 1 purlwise, K2) rep. to the last 2sts, sl 1 purlwise, K1.
4th row: K1, YF, sl 1 purlwise, YB, (K2, YF, sl 1 purlwise, YB) rep. to the last stitch, K1 ***
Rep. from *** to *** 6 times.
Shape Armholes: Keeping patt. in order, cast off 3sts at beg. of next 2 rows. Work 20 rows in patt. on the rem. sts. Break off B and cont. with C. K 1 row.
Next row: (K1, P1) rep. to the last stitch, K1.
Shape Shoulders: Cont. in rib and cast off 4sts at beg. of the next 4 rows (17sts).
Next row: (K2, inc. 1) rep. to the last 2sts, K2 (22sts).
K 6 rows for Collar then cast off on the next row. **

BACK LEGS AND BODY
With A cast on 15sts and work in g st.
K 8 rows, break off A. Join in C and K 10 rows. Work from ** to ** of Front Legs and Body.

HEAD
With A cast on 16sts for Front Head and work in g st, inc. 1 stitch each end of every 3rd row until 24sts.
Next row: Insert needle into the first stitch as if to K and wind yarn 3 times around right needle and 1st finger of left hand winding from right to left, draw all 3 loops through the stitch on the left needle, then transfer the 3 loops to the left needle and K all 3 loops tog., with the 2 loops on the 1st finger of left hand pull down making the loops firm (1 loop stitch made), K to last stitch, make 1 loop stitch in last stitch. Rep. the loop stitch in same way at each end of the foll. 3 alt. rows, then 2 loop sts at each end of the foll. 4 alt. rows.
Next row: K2 tog., K20, K2 tog. (22sts).
Next row: Loop stitch to end.
Next row: K and dec. 1 stitch at each end (20sts).
Rep. the last 2 rows twice (16sts) then K 2 rows. Cont. in loop stitch for Back Head and inc. 1 stitch each end of the next 8 rows (32sts).
Work 14 rows straight. Dec. 1 stitch each end of the next and every 3rd row until 16sts rem. K2 rows, then cast off on the next row.

HANDS AND ARMS
(2.) With A cast on 15sts and work in g st for 5 rows.
Next row: K7, (K1, P1, K1) all into the next stitch, K7 (17sts).
Next row: K8, (K1, P1, K1) all into the next st, K8 (19sts).
Next row: K9, (K1, P1, K1) all into the next stitch, K9 (21sts).
Knit 4 rows. Break off A, join in C and K 1 row.
Work 4 rows in rib of K1, P1.
Next row: Rib 3, (inc. 1, rib 2) rep. to end (27sts).
Work in patt. repeating from *** to *** until 42 rows. Cast off on the next row.

To make up:
Neatly join the Body pieces tog. on the wrong side leaving the cast on edge of Feet and cast off edge of Shoulders and Neck open. Fold the Hand and Arm pieces and join the underarm seam to within 1cm ($\frac{1}{2}$in) of top. Sew the Arms into the armholes. Turn out to the right side and fill firmly. Fill Legs from lower edge and join Feet, then fill Body from top and join Shoulder and Collar seams. Fill Head and sew Neck edge inside Collar. Cut out features and sew in position on Face. With coloured yarn work buttonhole stitch round curtain rings then sew to side of Head.

Daisy Flower Garden Puppet

you will need

Marriner Aristocrat Superwash Double Knitting Pure New Wool (machine washable)
–1 ball 25g Main Colour (MC)
–1 ball 25g Contrast Colour (CC)
Pair No 9 Aero Needles
Small piece of red felt

tension

24sts and 32 rows to 10.2cm (4ins) over stocking stitch (st st)

instructions

CUFF
With MC and needles cast on 40sts.
1st row: (K2, P2) rep. to end.
Rep. last row until 18 rows altog.
Cont. in st st and work 18 rows.
Tie a marker each end of last row.
Next row: Knit 20sts and sl these 20sts on to a holder. K rem. 20sts.
Cont. on last 20sts and work 17 rows.
Shape Nose:
1st row: K1, K2 tog., K to last 3sts, K2 tog., K1.
2nd row: P.
3rd and 4th rows: As 1st and 2nd rows.
5th row: As 1st row (14sts).
6th row: P1, P2 tog., P to last 3sts., P2 tog., P1.
7th row: As 1st row.
8th row: As 6th row (8sts).
9th row: K3 tog., K2 tog., K3 tog. (3sts).
10th row: P3 tog. and fasten off.
Return to 20sts on holder, sl them on to needle, join yarn at inner edge and P 1 row. Work 8 rows

in st st ending on a P row.
Shape Nose: As other side.

MOUTH

With CC and needles cast on 2sts.
1st row: K.
2nd row: K and inc. 1 stitch in each stitch (4sts).
3rd row: K.
4th row: K1, inc. 1 stitch in next 2sts, K1 (6sts).
5th row: K.
6th row: K1, inc. 1 stitch in next stitch, K to last 2sts, inc. 1 stitch in next stitch, K1 (8sts).
Rep. 5th and 6th rows until 16sts.
Cont. in g st until 32 rows from beg. (16 ridges). Tie in a marker each end of last row.
Work 10 more rows (5 more ridges) then proceed as follows:
1st row: K1, K2 tog., K to last 3sts, K2 tog., K1.
2nd row: K.
Rep. 1st and 2nd rows until 6sts rem.
Next row: (K3 tog.) twice (2sts).
Next row: K2 tog. and fasten off.

To make up:
With wrong side of work facing and using a flat seam (see page 20), join from beg. of cuff to row marked with ties. Hold mouth to inside of body making sure that markers on mouth and on body match and neatly sew these edges tog.

INNER FRILL: With CC and needles cast on 5sts.
1st row: K.
2nd row: K2, YF, K3.
3rd row: K4, YF, K2.
4th row: K3, YF, K4.
5th row: K5, YF, K3.
6th row: Cast off 4sts, K5.
Rep. these 6 rows 14 times more.
Cast off on next row.

OUTER FRILL: With CC and needles cast on 42sts and K 4 rows.
5th row: K1, * insert needle through next stitch, (YON and first 3 fingers of left hand) 3 times then YON again, pull 4 loops through stitch, sl on to left hand needle and K tog., rep. from * to last stitch, K1.
6th row: K.
Cast off on next row.

To finish off:
Gather straight edge of inner frill, place inside outer frill and with sl st sew in position as illustrated. Cut eyes from felt and attach to face.
You might like to make other garden puppets like Wilfred Worm and Franklin Frog pictured with Daisy Flower.

Long Halter-neck Dress

you will need

2 balls 20g Marriner Bouquet Double Knitting Approx. 60% Courtelle 40% Nylon (machine washable)
Pair No 9 Aero Needles

measurements

Chest – 23cm (9ins)
Length – 30.5cm (12ins)

tension

24sts and 32 rows to 10.2cm (4ins) over stocking stitch (st st)

instructions

(Worked in one piece to neck shaping.) Cast on 70sts, work 4 rows in st st.
Next row: K1, (YF, K2 tog.) rep. to last stitch, K1 (fold of hem).
Proceed for patt. as follows:
1st row: P.
2nd row: K.
3rd row: P.
Rep. 2nd and 3rd rows twice.
8th row: K1, (K2 tog., YF, K4) rep. to the last 3sts, K2 tog., YF, K1.
9th row: P.
10th row: K.
11th row: P.
Rep. 10th and 11th rows twice.
16th row: K1, (K3, K2 tog., YF, K1)
rep. to the last 3sts, K3.
Rep. last 16 rows inclusive for patt.
Cont. in patt. until work measures 15cm (6ins) from fold of hem ending on 1st row of patt. Keeping patt. in order dec. 1 stitch each end of the next row then every foll. 4th row until 54sts rem. ending on a P row.
Cont. in st st only. Cast off 12sts at beg. of next 2 rows (30sts).
Shape Halter Neck:
Next row: K2 tog., K 13sts, turn (leave rem. sts on a holder).
Next row: P to last 2sts, P2 tog.
* Next row: K2 tog., K to last 2sts, K2 tog. tbl.
Next row: P.
Rep. last 2 rows until 3sts rem. ending on a P row.
Work 6 rows then cast off on next row *.
Ret. to the rem. 15sts, join in yarn at Neck edge, K to last 2sts, K2 tog. tbl.
Next row: P2 tog., P to end.
Finish from * to *.

To make up:
Lightly press work on wrong side. Using a small backstitch (see page 18) sew back seam. Press seam open. Fold hem at fold of hem row to inside and sl st (see page 18) down.

To finish off:
With 6 strands of yarn make one plait 44cm (17¼ins) long and 2 plaits 29cm (11½ins) long. With a sl st and beg. at Centre Back, attach longer plait to back of dress, and around armholes and neck. Attach one of each short plait to each shoulder for tie.

Long-line Cardigan

you will need

2 balls 20g Marriner Bouquet
4 Ply. Approx. 60% Courtelle
40% Nylon (machine washable)
Pair No 11 Aero Needles
Pair No 12 Aero Needles
4 buttons

measurements

Chest – 23cm (9ins)
Length – 16.5cm ($6\frac{1}{2}$ins)
Sleeves – 8cm ($3\frac{1}{4}$ins)

abbreviations

Cr 2: Cross 2sts: Knit 2nd stitch then first stitch and slip both sts off needle tog.

tension

30sts to 7.6cm (3ins) and 26 rows to 6.4cm ($2\frac{1}{4}$ins) over patt.

instructions

BACK
With No 12 needles cast on 48sts and work in rib of K1, P1 for 6 rows. Change to No 11 needles and proceed in patt. as follows:
1st row: (K1, P1, K2, P1, K1, P1) rep. to last 6sts, K1, P1, K2, P1, K1.
2nd row: (K2, P2, K2, P1) rep. to last 6sts, K2, P2, K2.
Rep. last 2 rows once.
5th row: (K1, P1, Cr 2, P1, K1, P1) rep. to last 6sts, K1, P1, Cr 2, P1, K1.
6th row: (K2, P2, K2, P1) rep. to last 6sts, K2, P2, K2.
Rep. last 6 rows inclusive.
Cont. in patt. until work measures 11.5cm ($4\frac{1}{4}$ins) ending on a 2nd row.
Shape Raglans: Keeping patt. in order cast off 3sts at beg. of next 2 rows (42sts).
* Next row: K2 tog., work to last 2sts, K2 tog. tbl.
Next row: P2 tog., work to last 2sts, P2 tog.
Next row: Work to end.

Next row: P2 tog., work to last 2sts, P2 tog.
Next row: K2 tog., work to last 2sts, K2 tog. tbl.
Next row: Work to end.*
Rep. from * to * twice (18sts) then cast off in patt. on next row.

LEFT FRONT
** With No 12 needles cast on 22sts and work in rib of K1, P1 for 6 rows. Change to No 11 needles and proceed in patt. as follows:
1st row: (P1, K1, P1, K2, P1, K1) rep. to last stitch, P1.
2nd row: (P1, K2, P2, K2) rep. to last stitch, P1.
Rep. last 2 rows once.
5th row: (P1, K1, P1, Cr 2, P1, K1) rep. to last stitch, P1.
6th row: (P1, K2, P2, K2) rep. to last stitch, P1.
Rep. last 6 rows inclusive for patt.
Cont. in patt. until work measures 11.5cm (4¼ins) ** ending on a 2nd row.
Shape Raglan and Neck:
*** 1st row: Keeping patt. in order cast off 3sts, work to end (19sts).
2nd row: Work to end.
3rd row: Work 2 tog., work to end.
4th row: Work to last 2sts, work 2 tog. (17sts).
5th row: As 4th row.
6th row: As 4th row (15sts).
7th row: As 3rd row.
8th row: As 3rd row (13sts).
Rep. 3rd to 7th rows inclusive until 2sts rem., K2 tog., fasten off.***

RIGHT FRONT
Work from ** to ** of Left Front ending on a 3rd row. Finish from *** to *** of Left Front.

SLEEVES
With No 12 needles cast on 20sts and work in rib of K1, P1 for 6 rows.
Change to No 11 needles and proceed as follows:
1st row: (K1, P1) rep. to end.
2nd row: (P1, K1) rep. to end.
Rep. 1st and 2nd rows inclusive for patt. Inc. 1 stitch each end of next then every foll. 6th row until 26sts. Cont. until work measures 8cm (3¼ins). Keeping patt. in order cast off 3sts at beg. of next 2 rows (20sts). Dec. 1 stitch each end of next row then every alternate row, until 4sts rem. Work 1 row, then cast off in patt. on next row.

To make up:
Press work on wrong side. Using small backstitch (see page 18) sew Raglan, side and Sleeve seams. Press seams open.
Band for Fronts and back Neck:
With No 12 needles cast on 5sts.
**** 1st row: (K1, P1) rep. to last stitch, K1.
2nd row: (P1, K1) rep. to last stitch, P1.
Rep. 1st and 2nd rows once.
5th row: K1, K2 tog., YRN, P1, K1.
Rep. 2nd row once then rep. 1st and 2nd rows twice.****
Rep. from **** to **** 3 times.
Cont. in rib until Band, slightly stretched, measures 37.5cm (14¾ins) then cast off ribwise on next row.

To finish off:
Using a small backstitch neatly attach Band. Sew on Buttons (see page 20).

Trousers

you will need

2 balls 20g Marriner Bouquet 4 Ply. Approx. 60% Courtelle 40% Nylon (machine washable)
Pair No 10 Aero Needles
Pair No 12 Aero Needles
Elastic

measurements

Waist – 20cm (8ins)
Length of Inside Leg of Pants – 15cm (6ins)

tension

28sts and 37 rows to 10.2cm (4ins) over st st.

instructions

RIGHT LEG
With No 12 needles cast on 44sts and K 4 rows.
Change to No 10 needles and st st.
Cont. until work measures 10.2cm (4ins) (38 rows).
Next row: K2 tog., K to the last 2sts, K2 tog.
Work 5 rows: Rep. the last 6 rows twice (38sts).
Next row: K2 tog., K to the last 2sts, K2 tog.
Next row: P.
Rep. the last 2 rows twice (30sts).
Work 2 rows.
Next row: K2 tog. K to the last 2sts, K2 tog. (30sts).
Work 9 rows (ending on a P row).
Next row: K.
Rep. the last row 5 times then cast off on the next row.

LEFT LEG
Work as Right Leg.

To make up:
Lightly press work on the wrong side. Using a small backstitch (see page 18) sew inside Leg seams for 15cm (6ins) then sew Front and Back seams tog. Press seams open. Join elastic and attach to waistband using a herringbone stitch for casing.

Scarf Hat

you will need

8 balls 25g Marriner Aristocrat Superwash Double Knitting Pure New Wool (machine washable)
Pair No 9 Aero Needles
1 Aero Cable Needle

tension

23sts and 29 rows to 10.2cm (4ins) over rib pattern

measurements

183cm (72ins) long x 18.5cm ($7\frac{1}{4}$ins) wide

abbreviations

CT6: Cross two of 6sts: Sl next 4sts on to Cable Needle to back of work, K2, transfer 2 purl sts from Cable Needle on to left needle and P them, then K2 from Cable Needle.

instructions

With No 8 needles, cast on 54sts.
1st row: (K2, P2) rep. to last 2sts, K2.
2nd row: (P2, K2) rep. to last 2sts, P2.
Rep. 1st and 2nd rows 6 times.
* 15th row: (CT6, P2) rep. to last 6sts, CT6.
16th row: (P2, K2) rep. to last 2sts, P2.
Rep. 1st and 2nd rows 3 times then 15th and 16th rows once. *
Cont. in rib until work measures 65.5cm ($25\frac{3}{4}$ins).
Work from * to * once then cont. in rib until work measures 114cm (45ins) ending on a 2nd row.
Work from * to * once then cont. in rib until work measures 173cm (68ins) ending on a 2nd row.
Work from * to * once then work 14 rows in rib.
Cast off ribwise on next row.

To make up:
Lightly press on wrong side. Fold Scarf in half having 2 centre cable panels facing for Hat. Using small backstitch (see page 18) sew from centre fold to cable panel on one side only, carefully rounding corner at fold.

Scarf and Mittens

you will need

Marriner Aristocrat Superwash Double Knitting Pure New Wool (machine washable)
– 6 balls 25g Main Colour (MC)
– 1 ball 25g First Contrast (FC)
– 1 ball 25g Second Contrast (SC)
Pair No 9 Aero Needles

measurements

Scarf: 18cm (7ins) wide x 137cm (54ins) long
Mittens: To fit 10 to 12 years

tension

24sts to 10.2cm (4ins) and 8 rows to 2.5cm (1in)

instructions

Instructions for scarf:
With MC cast on 42sts and K6 rows.
Next row: K.
Next row: K3, P to last 3sts, K3.
Rep. last 2 rows inclusive.
Work 4 rows MC * 2 rows FC, 6 rows SC, 2 rows FC *, 12 rows MC.
Work from * to * once. With MC only cont. until work measures 123cm (48½ins) or length required ending on wrong side of work.
Work from * to * once, then with MC work 12 rows.
Work from * to * once, then with MC work 6 rows.
With MC K 6 rows, then cast off on next row.

Instructions for mittens:

RIGHT HAND
* With MC cast on 46sts and work in rib of K1, P1 for 8 rows.
Cont. in st st and work 2 rows in FC.
** Next row: With SC dec. 1 stitch each end of row.
Work 3 rows.
With FC work 2 rows.**
Next row: With MC dec. 1 stitch each end of row (42sts).
Work 3 rows.
With FC work 2 rows.
Rep. from ** to ** once (40sts).
Next row: With MC dec. 1 stitch each end of row (38sts).
Work 19 rows*.
Proceed for Thumb as follows:
1st row: K26, turn, cast on 4sts.
2nd row: P11, turn, cast on 3sts.
*** 3rd row: K14, turn.
4th row: P14, turn.
Rep. 3rd and 4th rows 6 times.
Next row: (K2 tog.) rep. to end.
Break yarn leaving a length, thread through rem. 7sts and sew seam.
With right side facing join in yarn at base of thumb, pick up and K 7sts on base then K rem. sts (38sts).
Next row: P.
Work 20 rows (adjust length at this point if required).
1st row: (K2 tog., K15, sl 1, K1, psso) twice (34sts).
2nd and alt. rows: P.
3rd row: (K2 tog., K13, sl 1, K1, psso) twice (30sts).
5th row: (K2 tog., K11, sl 1, K1, psso) twice (26sts).
7th row: (K2 tog., K9, sl 1, K1, psso) twice (22sts).
9th row: (K2 tog., K7, sl 1, K1, psso) twice (18sts).
11th row: (K2 tog., K5, sl 1, K1, psso) twice (14sts).
Slip 7 sts on to one needle, place 2 needles tog., break yarn and graft (follow instructions page 16) sts tog. Sew sides ***

LEFT HAND
Work as Right Hand from * to *
Proceed for Thumb as follows:
1st row: K19, turn, cast on 3sts.
2nd row: P10, turn, cast on 4sts.
Work from *** to *** of Right Hand.

To make up:
Sew side seams and press seams.

Pullover

you will need

6 (7:8) balls 25g Marriner Aristocrat Superwash Double Knitting Pure New Wool (machine washable)
Pair No 9 Aero Needles
Pair No 11 Aero Needles
Set of four No 11 Aero Needles
Cable Needle

abbreviation

C6: Cable 6sts: Slip next 3sts on to Cable Needle and leave at front of work, K3 then K 3sts from Cable Needle.

measurements

Chest – 66, (71:76) cm/ 26, (28:30) ins
Length – 37, (40:45) cm/ 14¾, (15¾:17¾) ins

tension

24sts and 32 rows to 10.2cm (4ins) over stocking stitch

instructions

BACK
With No 11 needles cast on 84, (90:96) sts and work in rib of K1, P1 for 14 rows.
Change to No 9 needles and proceed as follows:
1st row: (right side) K10, (4:7) sts, P2, C6, P2, (K8, P2, C6, P2) rep. 2, (3:3) times, K10, (4:7) sts.
2nd row: P10, (4:7) sts, K2, P6, K2, (P8, K2, P6, K2) rep. 2, (3:3) times, P10, (4:7) sts.
3rd row: K10, (4:7) sts, P2, K6, P2, (K8, P2, K6, P2) rep. 2, (3:3) times, K10, (4:7) sts.
* Rep. 2nd and 3rd rows twice, 2nd row once, 1st row once, then 2nd and 3rd rows once *.
Rep. from * to * (8 rows) inclusive for patt.
Cont. until work measures 22, (23:23.5) cm/$8\frac{3}{4}$, ($9:10\frac{1}{4}$) ins ending on wrong side of work.
Shape Armholes: Keeping patt. in order cast off 6, (6:7) sts. at beg. of the next 2 rows.
Dec. 1 stitch each end of next then every alternate row until 62, (68:72) sts. rem.**
Cont. in patt. until Armholes measure 15, (17:19) cm/6, ($6\frac{3}{4}:7\frac{1}{2}$) ins on straight ending on wrong side of work.
Shape Shoulders: Cast off at beg. of next and every row 7 sts 4 times, 5, (7:8) sts. twice, leave rem. 24, (26:28) sts. on a holder for back Neck.

FRONT
Work as Back to **.
Cont. in patt. until Armholes measure 6.5, (8:9.6) cm/$2\frac{1}{2}$, ($3\frac{1}{4}:3\frac{3}{4}$) ins on straight ending on wrong side of work.
Shape Neck:
Next row: Work 35, (39:41) sts, leave last 12, (14:14) sts just worked onto a holder for centre Front, work to end.
Cont. on the last 25, (27:29) sts.
Next row: Work to last 2sts, P2 tog.
Next row: K2 tog., work to end.
Rep. last 2 rows once.
Work 3 rows.
Next row: K2 tog., work to end.
Rep. last 4 rows 1, (1:2) times (19:21:22 sts).
Cont. until Armhole measures same as Back ending at Armhole edge.
Shape Shoulder: Cast off at beg. of next and every 2nd row 7 sts twice, 5, (7:8) sts once. Ret. to rem. sts, join in yarn at Neck edge, work 2 tog. Work to end.
Finish to correspond with other side.

To make up:
Press work on wrong side. Using small backstitch sew Shoulders, press seams open.
NECK BAND: With set of No 11 needles and right side of work facing beg. at Left Shoulder neatly pick up and knit 28, (30:30) sts each side of Front Neck, knit the 12 (14:14) sts from Centre Front holder and 24 (26:28) sts from Back Neck holder 92 (100:102) sts.
Work in rib of K1, P1 for 8 rounds then cast off loosely on next round.

To finish off:
Using a small backstitch sew sides, press seams open.
ARMHOLE BANDS: With set of No 11 needles neatly pick up and knit 80, (92:102) sts round Armholes and work 8 rounds in rib of K1, P1. Cast off loosely ribwise on next round.

Shoulder Bag

you will need

Marriner Aristocrat Superwash Double Knitting Pure New Wool (machine washable)
–6 balls 25g Main Colour (MC)
–3 balls 25g Contrast Colour (CC)
Pair No 9 Aero Needles
2 gold buckles
Small quantity cardboard
2 gold rings

measurements

Bag: 20cm (7¾ins) x 25cm (9¾ins)
Strap: 66cm (26ins) long

tension

24sts to 10.2cm (4ins) and 20 rows to 5.1cm (2ins) over moss stitch (m st)

instructions

MAIN PART OF BAG
With needles and MC cast on 63sts.
* 1st row: (K1, P1) rep. to last stitch, K1.
Rep. last row inclusive for patt.
Cont. until work measures * 66cm (26ins) then cast off on next row.

SIDE PANELS (4)
With needles and MC cast on 17sts.
Work from * to * 20cm ($7\frac{3}{4}$ins) then cast off on next row.

STRAPS AROUND BAG (2)
With needles and CC, cast on 9sts.
Work from * to * 1cm ($\frac{1}{2}$in).
**Next row: Work 4sts, YF, K2 tog., work to end ** (eyelet hole for attaching buckle).
Work from * to * 52cm ($20\frac{1}{2}$ins).
Rep. from ** to ** (eyelet hole for fastening buckle).
Work from * to * 57cm ($22\frac{1}{2}$ins) then cast off on next row.

SHOULDER STRAP
With needles and CC, cast on 9sts.
Work from * to * 66cm (26ins) then cast off on next row.

To make up:
Lightly press work on the wrong side. Using small backstitch join 2 sides and lower edge of side panels tog. to form two panels for sides of Bag. Cut cardboard to fit panels, rounding off corners and slide in through opening then with a sl st join opening.
Fold Bag and neatly fit side panels into position then with a sl st sew side panels to Bag, leaving 9sts from outer edge of Bag and beg. 9cm ($3\frac{1}{2}$ins) from lower edge of flap and strap.
With a sl st attach straps round Bag to end of flap, at the same time insert ring to top of Bag on shoulder strap. Attach buckles to end of strap and shoulder strap on ring.

Patchwork Blanket

you will need

Marriner Bouquet Chunky
Approx 60% Courtelle 40%
Nylon (machine washable)
–6 balls 40g First Colour (A)
–6 balls 40g Second Colour (B)
–6 balls 40g Third Colour (C)
–7 balls 40g Fourth Colour (D)
Pair No 6 Aero Needles

measurements

Motifs to measure 25.5cm (10ins) x 25.5cm (10ins)
Finished rug to measure 101.5cm (40ins) x 152cm (60ins)

tension

8sts to 5.1cm (2ins) and 22 rows to 10.2cm (4ins) over stocking stitch (st st)

instructions

GARTER STITCH SQUARE
(6) With A and needles cast on 37sts.
1st row: K.
Rep. last row until work measures 25.5cm (10ins). Cast off on next row.

STOCKING STITCH SQUARE
(6) With B and needles cast on 40sts.
1st row: K.
2nd row: P.
Rep. last 2 rows until work measures 25.5cm (10ins). Cast off on next row.

MOSS STITCH SQUARE
(6) With C and needles cast on 39sts.
1st row: (K1, P1) rep. to end.
Rep. last row until work measures 25.5cm (10ins). Cast off on next row.

FANCY STITCH SQUARE
(6) With D and needles cast on 48sts.

1st row: K.
2nd row: (K2 tog.) rep. to end.
3rd row: (K into front and back of stitch) rep. to end.
4th row: P.
Rep. last 4 rows until work measures 25.5cm (10ins). Cast off on next row.

To make up:
Lightly press squares on wrong side with a WARM iron and a DRY cloth. Using a small backstitch (see page 18) sew squares as shown on diagram. Press seams open.